Exploring the Dynamics of Online Messaging

C. P. Kumar
Reiki Healer & Author
Roorkee - 247667, India

Disclaimer

While every effort has been made to ensure the accuracy and completeness of the content in this book, the author cannot guarantee that the information contained herein is error-free, up-to-date, or suitable for every individual circumstance.

The author shall not be held liable or responsible for any errors or omissions in the content of the book, nor for any damages, or losses that may arise from any actions taken based upon the suggestions or contents presented in the book.

Readers are advised to use their own judgment and discretion in applying the information provided in this book, and to consult with qualified professionals before taking any action based on the contents of this book. The author disclaims any and all liability or responsibility for any actions taken or not taken based on the information contained in this book.

DEDICATION

To the Explorers of the Digital Frontier,

This book is dedicated to all those who navigate the intricate web of online messaging, seeking connection, understanding, and balance in the ever-evolving landscape of digital communication.

To the pioneers of the virtual realm, who have witnessed the evolution and growth of online messaging, recognizing its paramount importance in shaping contemporary communication.

To the adventurers who embrace the convenience and accessibility of instant communication across geographical boundaries, understanding the profound impact of 24/7 connectivity on relationships.

To the ambassadors of global connectivity, who build bridges through digital messages while navigating the cultural considerations that enrich our interconnected world.

To the storytellers who enhance communication through the vibrant medium of photos, videos, and documents, contributing to the richness of our digital interactions.

To those who strive for balance between the convenience of online messaging and the irreplaceable value of face-to-face communication, acknowledging the risks of over-reliance on the digital realm.

To the communicators who face the challenges of conveying emotions and intentions online, and to those who dedicate themselves to minimizing misunderstandings through thoughtful strategies.

To the empathetic souls who address emotional nuances in digital interactions, understanding the profound impact of building empathy through online messaging.

To the guardians of privacy, who navigate the risks of message interception and data theft, and advocate for the best practices ensuring online privacy.

To the vigilant defenders against online fraud, who detect and respond to evolving techniques and challenges in fraud prevention.

To the guardians of digital relationships who navigate the complex trails of cheating, seeking ways to prevent and address emotional infidelity in the vast expanse of the online world.

To the romantics who explore the advantages and disadvantages of digital relationships, navigating challenges and fostering genuine connections in the realm of online romance.

To those who manage online interactions through blocking, understanding the risks and potential drawbacks of such actions in the intricate dance of digital communication.

To the mindful navigators of digital distractions, who manage notifications and maintain productivity while embracing digital detox strategies for a healthier online existence.

To the guardians of mental well-being who delve into the positive and negative aspects of online messaging, offering strategies for maintaining a healthy digital balance in the pursuit of mental health.

To the advocates for safety and security measures, who encourage strong passwords and two-factor authentication, ensuring online safety through security best practices.

This dedication is a tribute to the collective spirit of exploration, understanding, and adaptability that defines those who venture into the dynamic world of online messaging. May your journey be filled with wisdom, empathy, and meaningful connections.

With heartfelt dedication,

C. P. Kumar

CONTENTS

PREFACE

In the vast expanse of the digital landscape, where every click, tap, and keystroke echoes across the interconnected web, the dynamics of online messaging have woven themselves into the very fabric of our contemporary existence. This book, "Exploring the Dynamics of Online Messaging", embarks on a journey through the intricate and evolving tapestry of digital communication, uncovering its nuances, challenges, and profound implications on our interconnected world.

As our lives become increasingly intertwined with the virtual realm, the evolution and growth of online messaging stand as a testament to the transformative power of technology in shaping the way we connect, communicate, and understand one another. This book seeks to be a guide through this transformative terrain, offering insights into the significance of online messaging in contemporary communication.

From the convenience and accessibility that instant communication provides across geographical boundaries to the impact of 24/7 connectivity on the delicate threads of relationships, each chapter is a portal into a specific facet of this digital frontier. We delve into the intricacies of global connectivity, exploring the ways in which online messaging serves as a bridge across cultures while navigating the cultural considerations that shape our digital interactions.

The narrative unfolds further as we examine the role of media sharing in enhancing communication, the risks associated with dependency on digital communication, and the delicate balance required to integrate face-to-face interactions with the conveniences of online messaging.

Miscommunication, a challenge inherent in the digital realm, takes center stage as we explore the complexities of conveying emotions and intentions online. Strategies to minimize misunderstandings pave the way for a more nuanced and empathetic form of digital communication.

Privacy concerns and the ever-looming specter of fraud take us into the realms of risk management, highlighting best practices for ensuring online privacy and tackling the evolving techniques and challenges in fraud prevention.

The book then ventures into the delicate territories of cheating in digital relationships and the multifaceted landscape of online romance, where advantages and disadvantages coexist, and genuine connections are fostered amid navigating challenges.

Blocking, often employed as a means of managing online interactions, is scrutinized for its risks and potential drawbacks, while discussions on distractions, digital detox strategies, and the impact of online messaging on mental health offer a holistic perspective on the individual's experience within the digital realm.

Finally, as we navigate through the diverse chapters, the conclusion beckons, summarizing key takeaways and emphasizing the importance of informed and mindful online communication. This journey is not just an exploration of the digital landscape but a guide for all those who seek to navigate it with wisdom, empathy, and a profound understanding of the dynamics that shape our interconnected world.

May this book serve as a compass for those who embark on this exploration, shedding light on the intricate pathways of online messaging and providing valuable insights that transcend the digital divide.

Welcome to the exploration.

C. P. Kumar
Reiki Healer & Author
Former Scientist 'G', National Institute of Hydrology
Roorkee - 247667, India
Web: https://www.angelfire.com/nh/cpkumar/virgo.html

In the rapidly evolving landscape of communication, online messaging has emerged as a pivotal force, shaping the way individuals connect, collaborate, and share information. This article delves into the multifaceted realm of online messaging, exploring its evolution, the diverse platforms that facilitate it, and its profound importance in contemporary communication.

Evolution and Growth of Online Messaging

The roots of online messaging can be traced back to the early days of the internet, where rudimentary forms of text-based communication were initiated. The advent of email marked a significant milestone, offering individuals a means to send asynchronous messages across the digital expanse. However, it was the rise of instant messaging (IM) that truly revolutionized the way people interacted online.

ICQ, one of the pioneering instant messaging platforms, introduced the concept of real-time communication over the internet in the late 1990s. This set the stage for the proliferation of IM services, with platforms like AOL Instant Messenger (AIM), MSN Messenger, and Yahoo Messenger dominating the landscape. These early systems laid the foundation for the more sophisticated online messaging platforms that we encounter today.

As technology advanced, so did the capabilities of online messaging. The introduction of multimedia elements such as images, videos, and emojis added a new layer of expressiveness to digital conversations. Moreover, the integration of voice and video calling features transformed online messaging into a comprehensive communication tool, bridging the gap between written and face-to-face interactions.

Online Messaging Platforms

The contemporary digital era is characterized by a diverse array of online messaging platforms, each catering to specific preferences, demographics, and communication styles.

1. Social Media Messaging

Platforms like Facebook Messenger, WhatsApp, and Instagram Direct Messaging have become integral parts of social media ecosystems. These services seamlessly integrate messaging with other features, facilitating communication within the context of broader social interactions.

2. Business Communication Tools

Slack, Microsoft Teams, and other enterprise-focused messaging platforms have revolutionized workplace communication. These tools enhance collaboration, streamline project management, and enable teams to communicate in real-time, irrespective of geographical constraints.

3. Multimedia Messaging Apps

Snapchat pioneered ephemeral messaging, allowing users to share images and videos that disappear after a set time. The success of Snapchat inspired features on other platforms, showcasing the dynamic nature of online messaging evolution.

4. Chatbots and AI-Powered Messaging

The integration of artificial intelligence into messaging platforms has given rise to chatbots that offer automated responses and assistance. These bots enhance user experience, providing quick information and resolving queries without human intervention.

Importance in Contemporary Communication

Online messaging has transcended the status of a mere convenience and has become an indispensable aspect of contemporary communication. Several factors contribute to its paramount importance.

1. Real-time Communication

Online messaging allows for instantaneous communication, breaking down the barriers of time and space. Whether it's connecting with friends, family, or colleagues, the ability to exchange messages in real-time has become a fundamental expectation in today's fast-paced world.

2. Accessibility and Convenience

The ubiquity of smartphones and internet connectivity has made online messaging accessible to a global audience. The convenience of sending messages anytime, anywhere fosters constant connectivity and strengthens relationships across borders.

3. Collaboration and Productivity

In the business realm, messaging platforms have transformed the way teams collaborate. Features like group chats, file sharing, and integrations with productivity tools contribute to streamlined workflows, enhancing overall organizational efficiency.

4. Social Connectivity

Online messaging platforms serve as hubs for social interaction, enabling individuals to stay connected with friends and family. This connectivity has become even more crucial in situations where physical distances or unforeseen circumstances limit face-to-face interactions.

5. Business Outreach and Marketing

For businesses, online messaging is a powerful tool for customer engagement, support, and marketing. Companies leverage messaging apps to communicate directly with customers, share updates, and provide personalized services, creating a more intimate and responsive brand-consumer relationship.

Conclusion

The exploration of online messaging reveals a dynamic landscape that has evolved significantly over the years. From the early days of basic text-based communication to the sophisticated, multimedia-rich platforms of today, online messaging has become an integral part of how individuals and businesses connect and communicate.

The diverse array of platforms, each tailored to specific needs, highlights the versatility and adaptability of online messaging. Whether it's social interactions, business collaborations, or automated assistance through AI-powered bots, the impact of online messaging is far-reaching and transformative.

As we navigate an increasingly digital world, the significance of online messaging in fostering real-time communication, enhancing accessibility, and facilitating collaboration cannot be overstated. It has not only changed the way we communicate but has also redefined the very fabric of human connection in the 21st century. As we continue to witness technological advancements, the dynamics of online messaging are likely to evolve, presenting new opportunities and challenges for individuals and businesses alike.

Introduction

The advent of online messaging has revolutionized the way we communicate, breaking down the barriers of time and space. In this era of instant gratification, convenience and accessibility have emerged as paramount factors shaping the dynamics of online messaging. This article delves into the multifaceted aspects of convenience and accessibility, exploring their impact on communication and relationships in the digital age.

Instant Communication Across Geographical Boundaries

One of the most significant contributions of online messaging is its ability to facilitate instant communication across geographical boundaries. Gone are the days when sending a message required days or even weeks to reach its destination. With the click of a button, messages traverse continents, connecting people in real-time. This newfound immediacy has not only transformed personal communication but has also revolutionized business interactions.

Consider the scenario of global business operations. Teams spread across different time zones can now collaborate seamlessly, breaking down the barriers of distance. The immediacy of online messaging allows for quick decision-making, fostering agility and efficiency in the business world. Furthermore, individuals separated by oceans can maintain relationships with ease, bridging the gap created by physical distance. Grandparents can share precious moments with their grandchildren, and friends can stay connected regardless of where life takes them.

Yet, this instant communication also brings challenges. The expectation of constant availability can lead to a sense of being constantly tethered to one's device. Striking a balance between staying connected and maintaining personal boundaries becomes crucial in navigating the complexities of instant communication.

24/7 Connectivity and Its Impact on Relationships

The rise of online messaging has ushered in an era of 24/7 connectivity. While this constant availability has undeniable benefits, such as immediate access to information and swift problem-solving, it also raises questions about the impact on relationships, both personal and professional.

In the realm of personal relationships, the ability to reach out at any time can foster a sense of closeness. Friends and family can share their triumphs and tribulations in real-time, creating a virtual presence even when physically apart. However, the flip side of this perpetual connectivity is the blurring of boundaries. The expectation of instant responses can create pressure and strain on relationships, as the line between personal and private time becomes increasingly thin.

Professional relationships, too, are not immune to the effects of 24/7 connectivity. The ability to communicate with colleagues and clients across different time zones can enhance collaboration and productivity. Yet, it also raises concerns about burnout and the erosion of work-life balance. The expectation to respond to work-related messages outside of traditional office hours can lead to a constant state of being on-call, impacting overall well-being.

Furthermore, the advent of social media and its integration into messaging platforms adds another layer to the 24/7 connectivity phenomenon. The curated nature of online personas and the constant stream of updates can contribute to a sense of inadequacy or FOMO (Fear of Missing Out). Balancing the benefits of staying informed with the potential negative impact on mental health becomes a delicate act in the age of constant connectivity.

Convenience Redefining Communication Norms

Convenience lies at the heart of online messaging, redefining communication norms and expectations. The ability to send messages at any time, coupled with features like read receipts and instant replies, has transformed the way we perceive and engage in conversations.

Consider the evolution of traditional letter writing into email communication and, subsequently, the instantaneous nature of messaging apps. The convenience of sending a quick text or voice message has become the new norm, challenging the formality of traditional communication. This shift has both positive and negative implications.

On the positive side, the convenience of online messaging allows for efficient communication, reducing the need for lengthy back-and-forths. Quick decision-making, coordination of plans, and sharing of information become seamless processes. However, this efficiency can also lead to a lack of nuance in communication. The brevity of messages may result in misunderstandings, as tone and context can be easily lost in the absence of face-to-face interaction.

Moreover, the convenience of online messaging extends to the realm of social interactions. Dating, for instance, has been profoundly influenced by the ease of connecting through apps and messaging platforms. While this accessibility broadens the pool of potential partners, it also introduces challenges related to authenticity and meaningful connection. The ease of swiping left or right can diminish the significance of genuine human connections, reducing relationships to a mere transaction.

Accessibility and Inclusivity in Communication

Online messaging has played a pivotal role in promoting accessibility and inclusivity in communication. The ability to connect with individuals regardless of physical or sensory limitations has been a transformative aspect of digital messaging.

For individuals with disabilities, online messaging provides a platform for communication that transcends traditional barriers. Text-based communication allows for the exchange of ideas, emotions, and information without relying on spoken words or physical presence. This inclusivity extends beyond disability to include individuals who may be geographically isolated or facing other challenges that limit their ability to engage in traditional forms of communication.

Moreover, the integration of features like voice-to-text and text-to-voice further enhances accessibility. These innovations cater to diverse communication preferences, making online messaging a versatile tool for a wide range of users. Inclusivity in communication becomes not just a goal but a reality, as technology evolves to accommodate the diverse needs of its users.

Conclusion

The dynamics of online messaging, shaped by convenience and accessibility, have undeniably transformed the way we communicate. Instant communication across geographical boundaries has brought people closer, fostering connections that transcend physical limitations. The 24/7 connectivity characteristic of digital messaging has redefined relationship norms, offering both opportunities for closeness and challenges related to boundaries and burnout.

Convenience, as a driving force, has streamlined communication processes, making them more efficient but also raising concerns about the depth of interpersonal connections. The accessibility of online messaging has become a beacon of inclusivity, breaking down traditional barriers and providing a platform for diverse voices.

As we navigate this evolving landscape of digital communication, it becomes essential to strike a balance between the benefits of convenience and accessibility and the potential pitfalls. The challenge lies in leveraging the power of online messaging to enhance connections without sacrificing the depth and authenticity that define meaningful communication. In this exploration of the dynamics of online messaging, the interplay between convenience and accessibility unfolds as a fascinating journey into the future of human connection.

Introduction

In the rapidly evolving landscape of the digital age, one phenomenon stands out as a cornerstone of our interconnected world - global connectivity. The advent of online messaging platforms has transcended geographical boundaries, facilitating instant communication and fostering unprecedented levels of global interaction. This article delves into the dynamics of global connectivity, exploring its multifaceted aspects and the transformative impact it has on our societies.

Building Global Connections Through Online Messaging

The rise of online messaging platforms has revolutionized the way individuals and businesses communicate across the globe. From the simplicity of text messages to the richness of multimedia content, these platforms offer a versatile means of connecting with people irrespective of distance. One of the key drivers of global connectivity is the accessibility of these platforms, providing users with the ability to communicate in real-time, share information, and collaborate seamlessly.

The business landscape, in particular, has witnessed a paradigm shift in the way international transactions and collaborations occur. Online messaging has become an integral tool for global enterprises, enabling swift and efficient communication among teams dispersed across different continents. This real-time connectivity not only enhances productivity but also fosters a sense of unity among diverse teams, breaking down the barriers imposed by physical distance.

Moreover, social interactions have been redefined through the lens of online messaging. Friendships are no longer constrained by geographical limitations, and families separated by oceans can share their daily lives with a simple tap on a screen. The democratization of communication has empowered individuals to build and nurture connections with people from different cultures and backgrounds, creating a global tapestry of relationships.

Cultural Considerations in Digital Communication

While the digital revolution has undeniably brought the world closer, it has also accentuated the importance of understanding cultural nuances in online communication. Cultural considerations play a pivotal role in shaping the dynamics of global connectivity, influencing how messages are perceived and interpreted.

Language, as a fundamental aspect of culture, becomes a crucial factor in digital communication. Online messaging platforms often transcend linguistic boundaries, supporting communication in multiple languages. However, the subtleties of expression, idioms, and cultural references can pose challenges in cross-cultural communication. As users navigate through the vast digital expanse, they must be mindful of cultural differences to avoid misunderstandings and misinterpretations.

Furthermore, the immediacy of online messaging amplifies the impact of communication, making it imperative to be sensitive to cultural norms. What may be considered acceptable in one culture could be perceived as offensive in another. Emoticons, GIFs, and memes, often used to convey emotions, may carry different connotations across cultures. A harmless gesture in one part of the world might be misconstrued elsewhere, highlighting the need for cultural literacy in the digital realm.

In the era of global connectivity, fostering inclusivity becomes paramount. Online messaging platforms should strive to accommodate diverse cultural practices, ensuring that users from different backgrounds feel acknowledged and respected. This inclusivity not only enhances the user experience but also contributes to the creation of a global digital community that celebrates diversity.

Challenges and Opportunities in Global Connectivity

While the benefits of global connectivity are evident, it comes with its own set of challenges. The digital divide, characterized by disparities in access to technology and the internet, poses a hurdle to achieving truly global connectivity. In some parts of the world, limited infrastructure and economic constraints hinder individuals from fully participating in the digital ecosystem, creating a digital divide that perpetuates inequality.

Moreover, the rapid pace of technological advancement brings forth security and privacy concerns. As individuals and businesses exchange sensitive information through online messaging, the need for robust cybersecurity measures becomes paramount. Global connectivity opens new avenues for cyber threats, necessitating a proactive approach to safeguarding digital communication channels.

However, challenges often present opportunities for innovation. Efforts to bridge the digital divide through initiatives that promote internet accessibility can unlock the untapped potential of millions, fostering more inclusive global connectivity. Similarly, advancements in cybersecurity technologies and practices can mitigate the risks associated with online messaging, ensuring a secure and trustworthy digital environment.

The Evolution of Online Messaging Platforms

As we navigate the dynamics of global connectivity, it is essential to trace the evolution of online messaging platforms. From the rudimentary Short Message Service (SMS) of the early mobile phones to the feature-rich messaging apps of today, the journey has been transformative.

The advent of smartphones marked a turning point in the evolution of online messaging. Apps like WhatsApp, Facebook Messenger, and WeChat emerged as pioneers, offering users the ability to send not just text but also multimedia content, voice messages, and conduct video calls. These platforms became integral parts of our daily lives, blurring the lines between personal and professional communication.

The integration of artificial intelligence (AI) has further elevated the capabilities of online messaging platforms. Chatbots powered by AI algorithms enable businesses to provide instant customer support, streamlining communication processes. Natural Language Processing (NLP) algorithms enhance the understanding of user inputs, making interactions with messaging platforms more intuitive and user-friendly.

The rise of ephemeral messaging, where content disappears after a set period, reflects changing user preferences and the demand for more private and transient forms of communication. Social media platforms incorporate messaging features, creating an all-encompassing digital experience where users can share moments, engage in conversations, and stay informed within a single platform.

Conclusion

Global connectivity, as facilitated by online messaging, has become the lifeblood of our interconnected world. The ability to communicate instantly and seamlessly across borders has redefined the way we connect, collaborate, and share our lives. As we navigate this digital landscape, it is imperative to embrace the opportunities and challenges that come with global connectivity.

Cultural considerations play a pivotal role in shaping the dynamics of online messaging, emphasizing the need for cultural literacy and inclusivity. While challenges such as the digital divide and cybersecurity concerns persist, they also present opportunities for innovation and progress. Initiatives to bridge the digital gap and advancements in cybersecurity technologies can pave the way for a more inclusive and secure digital future.

The evolution of online messaging platforms reflects the ever-changing needs and preferences of users. From simple text messages to sophisticated multimedia interactions, these platforms continue to evolve, driven by technological advancements and user expectations. As we explore the dynamics of online messaging in the context of global connectivity, it is clear that the journey is far from over. The future promises new horizons, innovations, and transformative experiences as we continue to connect and communicate in the digital age.

Introduction

In the era of digital communication, the dynamics of online messaging have undergone a transformative evolution. One of the pivotal aspects contributing to this evolution is the phenomenon of media sharing. The exchange of photos, videos, and documents has become an integral part of our online interactions, reshaping the way we communicate and share information. This article delves into the multifaceted aspects of media sharing, exploring its impact on communication dynamics in the digital realm.

Enhancing Communication Through Photos, Videos, and Documents

1. Visual Storytelling in the Digital Age

Media sharing has revolutionized the way we tell stories online. Photos and videos, in particular, have become potent tools for visual storytelling, transcending the limitations of traditional text-based communication. With the advent of smartphones equipped with high-quality cameras, individuals can effortlessly capture and share moments from their lives, offering a rich and immersive narrative to their audience.

The rise of social media platforms has further amplified the impact of visual storytelling. Instagram, Snapchat, and TikTok have become cultural phenomena, fostering a culture of instantaneous and engaging content sharing. Users can convey emotions, experiences, and ideas with a mere snapshot or a short video clip, creating a more profound connection with their audience than words alone could achieve.

2. Document Sharing: Collaborative Knowledge Building

Beyond visual media, the sharing of documents has empowered collaborative knowledge-building in unprecedented ways. Platforms like Google Drive and Dropbox allow users to seamlessly share and edit documents in real-time, fostering a collaborative environment irrespective of geographical distances. This has transformed the nature of remote work and collaborative projects, enabling teams to work efficiently and cohesively.

The ease of document sharing has also democratized information dissemination. Academic research, business reports, and educational resources can now be shared with a global audience effortlessly. This democratization of information not only accelerates the pace of innovation but also contributes to a more informed and interconnected global society.

Impact on the Richness of Digital Interactions

1. Emotional Expression and Connection

Media sharing has injected a new dimension of emotional expression into digital interactions. Emoticons are textual representations of facial expressions or gestures, often used to convey emotions in online communication, such as :-) for a smile. Emojis are small digital images or icons representing various objects, symbols, and facial expressions, used to convey emotions or ideas in electronic communication.

Emoticons and emojis, while serving as rudimentary forms of emotional expression, pale in comparison to the depth of sentiment conveyed through shared photos and videos. The ability to share moments of joy, sorrow, excitement, or nostalgia enables users to connect on a more profound level, transcending the limitations of text-based communication.

Social media platforms have become emotional canvases where users paint their experiences through shared media. From celebrating milestones to expressing solidarity during challenging times, the shared visual and auditory experiences create a shared emotional space that enhances the richness of digital connections.

2. Fostering Cultural Exchange

Media sharing has emerged as a powerful tool for fostering cultural exchange on a global scale. Through the lens of shared media, individuals can gain insights into diverse cultures, traditions, and perspectives. Social media platforms act as virtual bridges, allowing users from different corners of the world to share snippets of their lives, traditions, and cultural practices.

This cultural exchange is not limited to personal interactions. Brands and organizations leverage media sharing to communicate their values and narratives, transcending linguistic and cultural barriers. Advertisements and promotional campaigns are no longer confined to text; instead, they harness the emotive power of visuals and videos to resonate with a global audience.

Challenges and Considerations

However, the evolution of media sharing also raises ethical considerations and challenges. The ease of sharing visual content has led to concerns about privacy, digital manipulation, and the dissemination of misleading information. Striking a balance between the benefits of media sharing and the need for responsible online behavior becomes crucial in navigating the complex landscape of digital interactions.

Conclusion

The dynamics of online messaging have been profoundly shaped by the evolution of media sharing. The ability to share photos, videos, and documents has not only enriched the way we communicate but has also fostered a more connected and emotionally resonant digital landscape. From visual storytelling to collaborative knowledge-building, media sharing has become a cornerstone of digital interactions.

As we navigate the ever-evolving landscape of online communication, it is imperative to recognize the power and responsibility that come with media sharing. Balancing the advantages of enhanced communication with ethical considerations is key to harnessing the full potential of media sharing in shaping a more informed, connected, and culturally diverse digital society.

Introduction

In an era dominated by online messaging, the dynamics of communication have undergone a profound transformation. As we navigate the digital landscape, the question of dependency on virtual interactions versus the importance of face-to-face communication has become increasingly relevant. This article explores the intricate relationship between dependency and face-to-face communication in the context of online messaging, shedding light on the nuances that shape our interpersonal connections.

Balancing Online Messaging with In-Person Interactions

The rise of online messaging platforms has undeniably revolutionized the way we communicate. Instantaneous exchanges, global connectivity, and the convenience of asynchronous communication have become integral parts of our daily lives. However, the challenge lies in striking a delicate balance between the advantages of online messaging and the irreplaceable richness of face-to-face interactions.

While online messaging facilitates quick and efficient communication, it lacks the depth and nuance inherent in in-person conversations. Non-verbal cues, facial expressions, and body language play crucial roles in conveying emotions and establishing genuine connections. Striking this balance becomes pivotal in maintaining the authenticity of our relationships.

One of the key benefits of face-to-face communication is the ability to build trust and rapport. Meeting someone in person allows for a more comprehensive understanding of their personality, fostering a deeper connection. The shared experience of being physically present creates a unique bond that is challenging to replicate in the virtual realm. In professional settings, face-to-face interactions often enhance teamwork, collaboration, and innovation, as the richness of in-person communication enables a more nuanced exchange of ideas.

Risks of Over-Reliance on Digital Communication

Despite the convenience and efficiency offered by online messaging, an over-reliance on digital communication poses significant risks. One of the primary concerns is the potential erosion of genuine connections as interpersonal interactions become increasingly mediated by screens. Dependence on digital channels may lead to a sense of detachment and a lack of emotional resonance, hindering the development of authentic relationships.

Moreover, the constant barrage of digital messages can contribute to information overload and heightened stress levels. The pressure to respond promptly and maintain a virtual presence may lead to burnout, negatively impacting mental well-being. The absence of face-to-face communication can also contribute to a sense of isolation, as individuals may feel disconnected from the real-world social fabric.

In professional contexts, over-reliance on digital communication channels can lead to misunderstandings and misinterpretations. The absence of non-verbal cues in virtual exchanges increases the likelihood of communication breakdowns, potentially jeopardizing collaboration and teamwork. Face-to-face interactions, on the other hand, provide an opportunity for immediate clarification and resolution of issues, minimizing the risk of miscommunication.

The Impact on Personal Relationships

In the realm of personal relationships, the effects of dependency on digital communication are profound. The prevalence of social media and messaging apps has altered the dynamics of friendships and romantic connections. While these platforms facilitate constant connectivity, they also introduce new challenges, such as the tendency to prioritize online interactions over face-to-face time.

Couples, for instance, may find themselves caught in the trap of "phubbing" which refers to the act of snubbing or ignoring someone in a social setting by focusing on one's smartphone or other mobile device, rather than engaging in face-to-face conversation. This behavior not only diminishes the quality of interpersonal connections but may also lead to feelings of neglect and dissatisfaction. Face-to-face communication becomes crucial in maintaining emotional intimacy and addressing underlying issues that may be overlooked in the digital realm.

Family relationships, too, can be strained by excessive reliance on digital communication. Shared meals, family outings, and in-person conversations are fundamental to nurturing familial bonds. When these activities are replaced or diminished by virtual interactions, the sense of togetherness and emotional support may be compromised.

Conclusion

In the ever-evolving landscape of communication, finding a harmonious balance between online messaging and face-to-face interactions is imperative. While digital platforms offer unprecedented convenience and connectivity, they cannot replace the depth and authenticity of in-person communication.

Recognizing the risks of over-dependency on digital channels is crucial for maintaining the richness of our relationships, both personal and professional. Face-to-face interactions contribute to the fabric of human connection, fostering trust, understanding, and emotional resonance that transcend the limitations of virtual exchanges.

As we continue to explore the dynamics of online messaging, let us not forget the profound impact that face-to-face communication has on the texture of our lives. In navigating the digital age, the challenge lies not in abandoning one for the other but in weaving a tapestry that seamlessly integrates the best of both worlds.

Introduction

In the vast landscape of online communication, where messages traverse the digital realm at the speed of light, miscommunication lurks like a silent specter. As we navigate the intricate web of texts, emails, and instant messages, the nuances of face-to-face communication often get lost in translation. This article delves into the multifaceted world of miscommunication in online messaging, unraveling the challenges, exploring the intricacies of conveying emotions and intentions, and proposing strategies to minimize misunderstandings.

Challenges of Conveying Emotions and Intentions Online

1. The Absence of Non-Verbal Cues

One of the fundamental challenges in online messaging is the absence of non-verbal cues. In face-to-face conversations, gestures, facial expressions, and body language contribute significantly to the interpretation of messages. In the online realm, these cues are conspicuously absent, leaving room for ambiguity. A simple message devoid of context can be misinterpreted, leading to unintended consequences.

2. Textual Ambiguity and Tone Misinterpretation

Text, being inherently devoid of tone, can be a breeding ground for misinterpretation. The same sentence can carry different meanings based on the reader's perspective. The lack of vocal intonation makes it challenging to convey emotions accurately. A seemingly harmless message might be perceived as hostile, causing tension and discord.

3. Cultural and Linguistic Variations

In the global village of online communication, cultural and linguistic variations add another layer of complexity. Expressions that are innocuous in one culture might be offensive in another. Idioms, slang, and colloquialisms may not translate seamlessly, leading to confusion. Understanding the cultural nuances becomes crucial to fostering effective communication in the online sphere.

4. Psychological Distance

The virtual space often creates a psychological distance between individuals. In the absence of face-to-face interaction, people might feel detached and less accountable for their words. This perceived anonymity can result in a lack of empathy, making it easier to miscommunicate intentions and emotions.

Strategies to Minimize Misunderstandings

1. Explicit Communication

To mitigate the challenges of online messaging, explicit communication is paramount. Clearly articulating thoughts, feelings, and intentions leaves less room for misinterpretation. Emoticons and emojis can be judiciously employed to infuse a touch of emotion into the text, bridging the gap created by the absence of non-verbal cues.

2. Contextual Clarity

Providing context is a powerful tool in online communication. When messages are accompanied by relevant context, it enhances understanding and reduces the likelihood of miscommunication. Taking the time to explain the background or purpose behind a message helps in conveying the intended meaning effectively.

3. Mindful Language Use

Choosing words carefully is crucial in the online realm. Being mindful of the potential interpretations of words and phrases can prevent unintended conflicts. Avoiding ambiguous language and opting for straightforward, neutral terms can contribute to clearer communication.

4. Active Listening in the Digital Space

While online communication often emphasizes sending messages, active listening is equally important. Responding to messages with thoughtful consideration, seeking clarification when needed, and acknowledging the emotions conveyed by others can foster a sense of connection and minimize miscommunication.

5. Utilizing Video and Voice Messages

To overcome the limitations of textual communication, integrating video and voice messages can be invaluable. Seeing and hearing the speaker adds a layer of richness to the interaction, allowing for a more nuanced understanding of emotions and intentions. This can be particularly beneficial in contexts where tone is critical.

Conclusion

In the intricate tapestry of online messaging, miscommunication is an ever-present challenge. The absence of non-verbal cues, coupled with textual ambiguity and cultural variations, creates a fertile ground for misunderstandings. However, by adopting explicit communication, providing contextual clarity, using mindful language, practicing active listening, and incorporating visual and auditory elements, individuals can navigate the digital realm more effectively.

Understanding the dynamics of online messaging is an ongoing process. As technology continues to evolve, so too will the nuances of communication in the virtual space. By recognizing the challenges and implementing strategies to enhance clarity, we can hope to unravel the threads of miscommunication and foster more meaningful and authentic connections in the digital age.

Introduction

In the ever-evolving landscape of digital communication, the nuances of human interaction have taken on new dimensions. Online messaging, a ubiquitous form of communication in the contemporary world, brings with it both convenience and challenges. One significant facet of this digital dialogue is the phenomenon of impersonal. This article delves into the intricacies of impersonal communication, addressing its impact on emotional nuances, the potential for building empathy, and the broader dynamics shaping our online interactions.

Impersonal Communication Defined

Impersonal communication in the context of online messaging refers to exchanges that lack a deeply personal or emotional touch. Unlike face-to-face interactions where non-verbal cues play a crucial role, digital communication often relies solely on words. This absence of physical presence can lead to a sense of detachment, making the interaction feel impersonal.

Addressing Emotional Nuances in Digital Interactions

One of the primary challenges in online messaging is the difficulty of conveying and interpreting emotions accurately. In face-to-face conversations, tone of voice, facial expressions, and body language contribute significantly to the emotional context of a message. In the digital realm, however, these cues are often absent or diluted, leading to potential misunderstandings.

1. The Role of Emoticons and Emoji

Emoticons and emojis emerge as digital substitutes for non-verbal cues, attempting to bridge the emotional gap in online conversations. While they provide a certain degree of expressiveness, their subjective interpretation remains a challenge. What one person perceives as a friendly gesture might be seen as sarcasm by another.

2. The Impact of Textual Ambiguity

The concise nature of text messages can lead to ambiguity, as the absence of clarifying cues makes it challenging to discern the speaker's intent. This ambiguity can sometimes result in emotional disconnects, misinterpretations, or even conflicts.

Building Empathy through Online Messaging

While impersonal communication poses challenges, it also presents an opportunity to foster empathy in the digital sphere. Understanding and acknowledging these challenges can pave the way for more meaningful online interactions.

1. Active Listening in the Digital Realm

Empathy begins with active listening, even in the online realm. Encouraging individuals to express themselves freely and taking the time to understand their perspectives fosters a sense of connection. Digital platforms, through features like read receipts and typing indicators, can signal active engagement. Typing indicators are visual cues, such as a blinking ellipsis or other animation, that inform users in real-time when someone is actively typing a message in a digital communication platform, indicating that a response is in progress.

Being mindful of the words chosen in digital communication is crucial. Considering the potential impact of messages before sending them and being aware of the recipient's emotional state contribute to a more empathetic exchange. This mindfulness can counteract the impersonal nature of digital communication.

Creating an online environment where individuals feel comfortable expressing their thoughts and emotions without fear of judgment is essential. Building trust through consistent, supportive communication encourages openness and vulnerability, fostering deeper connections.

Conclusion

Impersonal communication in online messaging is a multifaceted phenomenon that challenges traditional notions of interpersonal connection. The digital realm, while lacking some of the sensory elements inherent in face-to-face interactions, offers unique opportunities for fostering empathy and understanding. By addressing the nuances of emotional expression, incorporating mindful communication practices, and encouraging openness, we can navigate the impersonal aspects of online messaging and cultivate more meaningful connections in the digital age.

As we continue to explore the dynamics of online messaging, it becomes evident that the evolution of communication technologies necessitates a parallel evolution in our understanding and approach to interpersonal relationships. Acknowledging the strengths and limitations of digital communication allows us to harness its potential for positive engagement and human connection.

Introduction

In the age of rapid technological advancements, online messaging has become an integral part of our daily lives, connecting people across the globe in an instant. While the convenience and efficiency of online communication are undeniable, it brings forth a myriad of privacy concerns that warrant careful consideration. In this article, we delve into the dynamics of online messaging, shedding light on the risks of message interception and data theft, exploring best practices for ensuring online privacy.

Risks of Message Interception and Data Theft

1. End-to-End Encryption and Its Limitations

One of the cornerstones of secure messaging is end-to-end encryption, which ensures that only the intended recipient can decipher the message. However, even with this advanced encryption, vulnerabilities still exist. Government agencies and malicious actors can exploit weaknesses in the encryption protocols, posing a threat to the confidentiality of sensitive information.

2. Metadata: The Silent Revealer

While the content of encrypted messages remains secure, metadata – information about the communication itself – often goes unnoticed. Metadata can unveil crucial details, such as the time, location, and parties involved in a conversation. Companies and third-party applications may use this metadata for targeted advertising, raising concerns about user privacy.

3. Phishing Attacks and Social Engineering

Beyond encryption vulnerabilities, users face the persistent threat of phishing attacks and social engineering. Cybercriminals employ sophisticated tactics to manipulate individuals into divulging personal information. Messages masquerading as trustworthy sources can lead unsuspecting users to click on malicious links or provide sensitive data, resulting in identity theft or financial losses.

4. Inadequate Security Measures of Messaging Apps

Not all messaging apps prioritize robust security measures. Some apps may store messages in an unencrypted format, leaving them susceptible to unauthorized access. Additionally, weak password policies and inadequate authentication methods can compromise the overall security of these platforms, making them easy targets for cyber threats.

Best Practices for Ensuring Online Privacy

1. Choose Secure Messaging Apps Wisely

Selecting a messaging app with a strong commitment to user privacy is the first line of defense. Apps that implement end-to-end encryption, regularly update security protocols, and have a transparent privacy policy should be prioritized. Signal, WhatsApp, and Telegram are notable examples of platforms that emphasize user privacy and security.

2. Regularly Update Software and Apps

Keeping software and messaging apps up-to-date is crucial for maintaining security. Developers release updates to address vulnerabilities and enhance security features. Neglecting these updates may expose users to known threats that have already been patched. Enabling automatic updates whenever possible ensures that users benefit from the latest security enhancements.

3. Employ Two-Factor Authentication (2FA)

Adding an extra layer of protection through two-factor authentication can significantly bolster the security of online messaging accounts. Even if login credentials are compromised, the need for a secondary authentication method acts as a deterrent for unauthorized access. Users should opt for apps that offer 2FA as part of their security features.

4. Be Wary of Phishing Attempts

Phishing is a cyber attack strategy in which attackers use deceptive emails, messages, or websites to trick individuals into revealing sensitive information, such as usernames, passwords, or financial details. The goal is to manipulate recipients into believing they are interacting with a trustworthy entity, often mimicking legitimate organizations, in order to gain unauthorized access to their personal or confidential data.

Vigilance is paramount in the face of phishing attempts. Users should scrutinize incoming messages, especially those containing links or requesting sensitive information. Authenticity verification, such as confirming the identity of the sender through alternative means, can prevent falling victim to phishing scams. Education and awareness campaigns play a vital role in empowering users to recognize and avoid such threats.

5. Review App Permissions

Messaging apps often request access to various device features and personal information. Users should review and understand the permissions requested by each app and limit access to only essential features. Granting unnecessary permissions may expose sensitive data and compromise privacy. Regularly auditing app permissions ensures that users maintain control over their personal information.

Conclusion

As online messaging continues to shape the way we communicate, it is imperative to address the associated privacy concerns. The risks of message interception and data theft are real and evolving, demanding proactive measures from both users and developers. By embracing secure messaging apps, staying informed about potential threats, and adopting best practices for online privacy, individuals can navigate the dynamic landscape of online messaging with confidence. Balancing the convenience of instant communication with a vigilant approach to security is the key to safeguarding our digital interactions in an era where privacy is increasingly under threat.

Introduction

In the digital age, where communication has seamlessly shifted to online platforms, the prevalence of fraud has become a significant concern. As the reliance on online messaging continues to grow, so does the need for robust fraud prevention mechanisms. This article delves into the intricacies of fraud prevention within the context of online messaging, exploring the methods used to detect and respond to fraudulent activities, the evolving techniques employed by cybercriminals, and the challenges that persist in this dynamic landscape.

Online Frauds

Online frauds encompass a wide range of deceptive practices orchestrated in the digital realm with the aim of unlawfully acquiring personal or financial information. Perpetrators often employ various tactics, including phishing emails, fake websites, and fraudulent online schemes, to trick individuals into divulging sensitive data such as passwords, credit card details, or social security numbers. These fraudulent activities exploit the anonymity and interconnected nature of the internet, posing a significant threat to individuals, businesses, and financial institutions alike. As technology advances, online frauds continue to evolve, necessitating ongoing efforts to enhance cybersecurity measures and raise awareness to protect users from falling victim to these malicious activities.

Detecting and Responding to Online Fraud

1. Machine Learning Algorithms in Fraud Detection

One of the cornerstones of effective fraud prevention is the utilization of machine learning algorithms. These algorithms analyze vast amounts of data, identifying patterns and anomalies that may indicate fraudulent behavior. By continuously learning and adapting to new tactics, machine learning algorithms play a crucial role in staying one step ahead of cybercriminals.

2. Behavioral Analysis for User Authentication

Beyond traditional methods of authentication, such as passwords and biometrics, behavioral analysis has emerged as a powerful tool in fraud prevention. By monitoring user behavior over time, systems can establish a baseline of normal activity. Deviations from this baseline, such as unusual login times or locations, trigger alerts for further investigation, preventing unauthorized access and fraudulent transactions.

3. Real-Time Monitoring and Alerts

The speed at which fraudulent activities can occur demands real-time monitoring and response. Systems equipped with real-time monitoring capabilities can detect suspicious behavior as it happens, allowing for immediate intervention. Automated alerts ensure that security teams can respond promptly, mitigating potential damage and preventing further unauthorized access.

Evolving Techniques and Challenges in Fraud Prevention

1. Social Engineering in Online Messaging

As technology advances, so do the tactics employed by cybercriminals. Social engineering, a technique that manipulates individuals into divulging confidential information, has become increasingly sophisticated in the realm of online messaging. Attackers may impersonate trusted entities or create convincing phishing messages, making it essential for users to be vigilant and for platforms to implement advanced security measures.

2. Deepfakes and Identity Theft

Deepfakes are realistic digital manipulations, often using AI, to create deceptive audio, video, or image content by replacing one person's likeness with another. They pose challenges due to their potential for malicious use in spreading misinformation and manipulating media.

The rise of deepfake technology poses a unique challenge in fraud prevention. Deepfakes use artificial intelligence to create realistic-looking videos or audio recordings of individuals, often for malicious purposes. Identity theft becomes more potent when cybercriminals can convincingly impersonate others in online messaging platforms, necessitating the development of advanced authentication methods to verify the legitimacy of users.

3. Cryptocurrency and Money Laundering

Cryptocurrency and money laundering are intertwined as digital currencies offer a degree of anonymity, making them attractive to criminals seeking to conceal the origins of illicit funds. While not inherently illegal, the pseudonymous nature of many cryptocurrencies can be exploited for money laundering purposes, facilitating the covert transfer of funds across borders without traditional banking scrutiny. Regulatory measures and advancements in blockchain analytics aim to mitigate these risks and enhance transparency within the cryptocurrency space.

The decentralized and pseudonymous nature of cryptocurrencies has made them an attractive tool for cybercriminals involved in fraud. Money laundering through cryptocurrencies poses a significant challenge for traditional financial institutions and law enforcement agencies. As online messaging platforms are often used to facilitate transactions, integrating robust measures to trace and prevent illicit financial activities becomes imperative.

4. Cross-Platform Attacks

Cross-platform attacks involve malicious activities targeting vulnerabilities across different operating systems or software ecosystems, aiming to exploit weaknesses in diverse platforms to compromise systems or data. These attacks often require adaptable strategies to breach the security of multiple platforms simultaneously.

In an interconnected digital ecosystem, cybercriminals exploit vulnerabilities across multiple platforms. Online messaging serves as a common entry point for these cross-platform attacks. Once access is gained through a compromised messaging account, cybercriminals can escalate their activities to other platforms, highlighting the need for integrated security solutions that span various digital environments.

Conclusion

As the landscape of online messaging continues to evolve, so must the strategies employed in fraud prevention. The integration of advanced technologies, such as machine learning, behavioral analysis, and real-time monitoring, plays a pivotal role in staying ahead of cybercriminals. However, the challenges are ever-present, with emerging techniques like deepfakes and social engineering demanding constant adaptation and innovation.

The collaborative efforts of individuals, businesses, and technology providers are essential in creating a secure online messaging environment. By fostering a culture of awareness, implementing cutting-edge security measures, and addressing the evolving nature of fraud, we can collectively build a resilient defense against the ever-present threats in the digital realm. As we navigate the complexities of online messaging, a proactive and collaborative approach to fraud prevention is paramount to safeguarding the integrity and security of our digital interactions.

Introduction

In the ever-evolving landscape of digital communication, relationships are increasingly shaped by online interactions. From social media platforms to messaging apps, the digital realm offers unprecedented connectivity. However, this connectivity comes with its own set of challenges, one of which is the issue of cheating in digital relationships. As our lives become more intertwined with the virtual world, the boundaries of fidelity are being tested in ways previously unimaginable. This article delves into the complex dynamics of cheating in digital relationships, examining the digital trails and discovery, addressing emotional infidelity online, and exploring ways to prevent and navigate these challenges.

Digital Trails and Discovery

Digital trails refer to the traces of online activities left by individuals as they interact with digital devices and services, creating a record of their behavior, preferences, and interactions across the internet. These trails, comprised of data such as search history, social media interactions, and online transactions, are often utilized for various purposes, including targeted advertising, user profiling, and personalized content delivery.

One of the unique aspects of digital relationships is the creation of electronic trails that can serve as a double-edged sword. On one hand, these trails provide a record of interactions, enabling couples to stay connected despite physical distances. On the other hand, they also serve as potential evidence of infidelity, leaving a trace of clandestine activities. The ease with which digital information can be stored and retrieved makes it challenging for individuals engaged in infidelity to conceal their actions completely.

Social Media and the Double-Edged Sword

Social media platforms, in particular, play a significant role in the dynamics of digital relationships. They provide a window into the lives of others and offer a platform for individuals to connect with a wide array of people. However, this increased connectivity can lead to unintended consequences. Digital trails on platforms like Facebook, Instagram, or Twitter can reveal interactions, likes, and comments that may raise suspicions or confirm suspicions of infidelity.

Moreover, the public nature of social media can amplify the consequences of digital infidelity. A seemingly harmless exchange between two individuals can quickly escalate into a public drama, affecting not only the individuals involved but also their broader social circles. The viral nature of online content adds a layer of complexity to the fallout of digital cheating, making it challenging to contain the repercussions.

Messaging Apps and Privacy Concerns

While social media may expose digital interactions to a broader audience, messaging apps offer a more private space for communication. Platforms like WhatsApp, Telegram, or Snapchat provide a level of intimacy that can foster emotional connections. However, this very privacy also makes it easier for individuals to engage in secretive conversations and activities.

Discovering digital infidelity often involves navigating through the labyrinth of private messages. Partners may find themselves facing moral dilemmas as they weigh the desire to respect privacy against the need for transparency in a relationship. The tension between trust and the fear of betrayal is heightened in the digital age, where personal boundaries are not just physical but extend into the virtual realm.

Preventing and Addressing Emotional Infidelity Online

As digital relationships become an integral part of modern life, addressing and preventing emotional infidelity online is crucial for maintaining healthy connections. Communication, trust, and setting boundaries are key elements in navigating the complexities of digital relationships.

1. Communication and Transparency

Open and honest communication is the cornerstone of any relationship, and this holds true in the digital realm. Couples need to establish clear expectations regarding digital boundaries and what constitutes inappropriate behavior online. Regular and transparent conversations about online activities can help build trust and create a shared understanding of acceptable behavior.

2. Building Trust in the Digital Age

Trust is fragile, and maintaining it in the digital age requires intentional effort. Partners should be proactive in sharing information about their online interactions, whether it be friendships or professional connections. Building trust involves not only being truthful but also being mindful of how one's actions may be perceived by the other person.

3. Setting Boundaries in the Virtual Space

Establishing boundaries is essential for preventing and addressing emotional infidelity online. Couples should have discussions about acceptable levels of privacy, the nature of online friendships, and the sharing of personal information. Setting clear boundaries helps create a framework for the relationship that respects both individuals' needs and expectations.

4. Seeking Professional Guidance

In some cases, addressing digital infidelity may require the assistance of a professional. Couples therapy, whether in-person or online, can provide a neutral space for partners to explore their concerns, improve communication, and work towards rebuilding trust. A therapist with expertise in digital relationships can offer valuable insights and guidance tailored to the challenges of the virtual world.

Conclusion

As online messaging continues to shape the landscape of modern relationships, the dynamics of fidelity are being redefined. The digital realm offers both opportunities for connection and challenges to the traditional boundaries of commitment. Navigating the complexities of cheating in digital relationships requires a thoughtful and proactive approach.

Understanding the implications of digital trails and the challenges of privacy in messaging apps is essential for couples to build trust and maintain healthy connections. Preventing and addressing emotional infidelity online involves open communication, building trust, setting clear boundaries, and, when necessary, seeking professional guidance. As we continue to explore the dynamics of online messaging, it is crucial to recognize the impact of digital interactions on the fabric of our relationships and work towards creating a healthy and secure digital space for connection and intimacy.

Introduction

In the rapidly evolving landscape of modern relationships, online romance has emerged as a significant facet of human connection. As technology continues to weave itself into the fabric of our daily lives, the way we form and maintain romantic connections has undergone a profound transformation. The digital realm offers a myriad of platforms and opportunities for individuals to engage in romantic pursuits, from dating apps to social media platforms. This article delves into the nuances of online romance, shedding light on its advantages and disadvantages, while also exploring strategies for navigating challenges and fostering genuine connections in the virtual space.

Dating Platforms

Dating apps, websites, and social media platforms have revolutionized the way people connect in the digital age. Popular dating apps include Tinder, Bumble, and OkCupid, which utilize swiping mechanisms and algorithms to match users based on their preferences. Websites like Match.com and eHarmony employ detailed profiles and compatibility tests to facilitate long-term relationships. Social media platforms such as Facebook and Instagram also play a role in dating, as users can connect with potential partners through friend networks or shared interests. Despite the convenience these platforms offer, users should navigate them with caution, considering privacy and safety concerns in the pursuit of meaningful connections.

Advantages of Digital Relationships

Global Connectivity and Diversity: One of the primary advantages of online romance lies in its ability to connect individuals across geographical boundaries. Dating apps and websites provide a platform where people from diverse backgrounds can interact and build connections that transcend physical limitations.

Access to a Diverse Pool of Potential Partners: The digital world widens the scope of romantic possibilities by introducing individuals to a vast pool of potential partners. This diversity allows people to explore relationships with those they might never have encountered in their offline lives.

Efficiency and Convenience: Online romance offers unparalleled efficiency and convenience. Through digital platforms, individuals can explore multiple connections simultaneously, saving time and effort compared to traditional dating methods.

Matching Algorithms and Compatibility: Many dating platforms utilize sophisticated algorithms to match individuals based on compatibility factors. This increases the likelihood of finding a suitable partner, as the algorithms consider shared interests, values, and preferences.

Initial Screening and Reduced Awkwardness: Online interactions allow individuals to screen potential partners before committing to a face-to-face meeting. This initial screening can reduce the awkwardness of first encounters, enabling people to establish a level of comfort before transitioning to in-person interactions.

Disadvantages of Digital Relationships

Superficiality and Image Crafting: A significant drawback of online romance is the potential for superficial connections. The curated nature of online profiles may lead individuals to present an idealized version of themselves, fostering unrealistic expectations and disappointment when reality fails to align with the digital persona.

Lack of Non-Verbal Cues: Digital communication lacks the richness of face-to-face interaction, as it eliminates crucial non-verbal cues such as body language and tone of voice. Misinterpretation of messages can occur, leading to misunderstandings and conflicts.

Over-reliance on Technology: In some cases, online relationships may suffer from an over-reliance on technology. The constant connectivity and reliance on messaging can impede the development of deeper emotional connections that often thrive through personal, offline interactions.

Privacy Concerns and Safety Risks: Engaging in online romance exposes individuals to potential privacy breaches and safety risks. *Catfishing* (act of creating a deceptive online persona to trick others into forming a relationship, typically for fraudulent or deceptive purposes), *identity theft* (the fraudulent acquisition and use of another person's personal information, such as their name, financial details, or Social Security number, typically for financial gain or to commit various forms of fraud), and online harassment are real concerns that can jeopardize the well-being of those seeking love in the digital realm.

Navigating Challenges and Fostering Genuine Connections

Communication Transparency: To build trust and authenticity in online relationships, communication transparency is essential. Being open and honest about intentions, expectations, and emotions can lay the foundation for a genuine connection.

Balancing Online and Offline Interaction: While online platforms facilitate initial connections, it is crucial to balance digital interactions with face-to-face encounters. Building a relationship in the offline world provides a more holistic understanding of a person beyond the confines of a digital profile.

Mindful Social Media Use: Social media plays a significant role in modern relationships. Being mindful of social media use and its impact on relationships is essential. Setting boundaries and respecting privacy can contribute to a healthier online romantic experience.

Cultivating Emotional Intelligence: Navigating the nuances of online romance requires a high level of emotional intelligence. Being attuned to one's own emotions and understanding the emotional cues of a partner can foster empathy and strengthen the emotional bond.

Seeking Shared Experiences: Creating shared experiences, even in the digital realm, can deepen the connection between individuals. Whether it's playing online games together, watching movies simultaneously, or participating in virtual activities, shared experiences contribute to the development of a shared history.

Conclusion

Online romance has become an integral part of the modern dating landscape, offering both advantages and challenges. While the digital realm provides unprecedented access to potential partners and efficient ways of connecting, it also presents risks such as superficiality and privacy concerns. Navigating the dynamics of online messaging in the context of romance requires a thoughtful approach, emphasizing transparency, communication, and a balance between online and offline interactions.

As technology continues to shape the way we form connections, understanding the intricacies of online romance becomes paramount. By acknowledging the advantages and disadvantages, and implementing strategies to navigate challenges, individuals can foster genuine connections that transcend the digital realm and contribute to meaningful, lasting relationships. Ultimately, online romance is a dynamic and evolving landscape that, when approached mindfully, has the potential to enhance and enrich the tapestry of human connection in the 21st century.

Chapter 12. Blocking and its Consequences

Introduction

In the age of digital communication, online messaging platforms have become integral to our daily lives, offering a convenient and instantaneous means of connecting with others. However, as the digital realm evolves, so do the challenges associated with managing online interactions. One prevalent aspect of this dynamic is the practice of blocking, a feature that allows users to restrict or sever communication with specific individuals. This article delves into the complexities of blocking within the context of online messaging, exploring its implications, risks, and potential drawbacks.

Managing Online Interactions Through Blocking

Blocking, at its core, is a mechanism that empowers users to regulate their online social circles. Whether it's on social media platforms, messaging apps, or other digital spaces, individuals can exercise control over their online presence by selectively blocking others. This tool is often employed for a variety of reasons, including but not limited to personal boundaries, protection from harassment, or simply the desire for a more curated online experience.

One significant advantage of blocking is its ability to offer a sense of agency and security to users. By implementing this feature, individuals can shield themselves from unwanted attention, offensive content, or even potential threats. This control over one's digital environment can contribute to a more positive online experience, fostering a sense of safety and comfort.

However, the use of blocking is a double-edged sword, as it introduces a range of consequences that extend beyond the immediate termination of communication.

Risks and Potential Drawbacks of Blocking

1. Communication Breakdown

Blocking severs the direct line of communication between individuals, potentially leading to misunderstandings and misinterpretations. What might have been a minor disagreement or a simple misunderstanding can escalate when the ability to engage in dialogue is abruptly cut off. The absence of communication channels can hinder conflict resolution and impede the potential for mutual understanding.

2. Echo Chambers and Polarization

Echo chambers are online or social environments where individuals are predominantly exposed to information, opinions, or ideas that align with their existing beliefs, reinforcing and amplifying their own perspectives while limiting exposure to diverse viewpoints or dissenting opinions.

While blocking offers users the ability to curate their online experience, it also contributes to the creation of echo chambers. By selectively blocking dissenting opinions or contrasting viewpoints, users may inadvertently isolate themselves within a bubble of like-minded individuals. This echo-chamber effect can reinforce pre-existing beliefs, fueling polarization and limiting the diversity of perspectives in online discourse.

3. Social Repercussions

The act of blocking can have social repercussions that extend beyond the digital realm. In close-knit communities or social circles, blocking someone may lead to tension, drama, or the alienation of the blocker from a wider social group. The fallout from such actions can affect relationships, both online and offline, with potential consequences for one's social standing and mental well-being.

4. Impact on Mental Health

Blocking, especially in the context of social media, can take a toll on mental health. Constant exposure to a curated, idealized online world can lead to feelings of inadequacy or loneliness for those on the receiving end of a block. Moreover, the act of blocking itself may induce guilt or anxiety for the person implementing it, as it involves making a conscious decision to exclude someone from their digital life.

5. Potential for Abuse

While blocking is a valuable tool for personal safety, it can also be misused. In certain cases, individuals may resort to blocking as a means of control or manipulation, stifling dissent and avoiding uncomfortable conversations. This misuse of blocking can contribute to a toxic online environment and hinder the free exchange of ideas.

Conclusion

The dynamics of online messaging are complex and multifaceted, with blocking emerging as a powerful tool for individuals to shape their digital experiences. However, the consequences of blocking extend beyond the immediate cessation of communication, impacting relationships, social dynamics, and mental well-being.

As users navigate the digital landscape, it is essential to approach blocking with a nuanced understanding of its implications. Striking a balance between self-preservation and open communication is key to fostering a healthy online environment. By acknowledging the risks and potential drawbacks of blocking, users can make informed decisions that contribute to a more inclusive and empathetic online community.

In the ever-evolving world of online messaging, exploring these dynamics is crucial for cultivating a digital space that promotes connection, understanding, and positive interaction.

Introduction

In an era dominated by online communication, the dynamics of messaging have evolved rapidly, bringing both convenience and challenges. One pervasive challenge is the constant barrage of distractions that accompany the digital realm. As individuals immerse themselves in the world of online messaging, the ability to stay focused becomes paramount. This article delves into the intricacies of distractions, offering insights into managing notifications, maintaining productivity, implementing digital detox strategies, and ultimately, finding a balance in the realm of online messaging.

Managing Notifications and Maintaining Productivity

The incessant *pings* (electronic signals or messages sent between devices), *dings* (short, sharp, metallic sounds or notifications), and *vibrations* (rhythmic oscillations or movements denoting the tactile feedback generated by a device to alert the user) emanating from our devices can be a double-edged sword. While notifications keep us connected, they also pose a significant threat to our productivity.

1. The Impact of Notifications

Notifications serve as a gateway to information, providing real-time updates on messages, emails, and social media interactions. However, their constant bombardment can lead to a fragmented focus, disrupting workflow and hindering concentration. Recognizing the impact of notifications is the first step in managing their influence on our productivity.

2. Setting Boundaries

Establishing boundaries is crucial for managing notifications effectively. Designate specific times to check messages and emails rather than responding immediately to every alert. By creating intentional intervals for communication, you regain control over your time and reduce the disruptive nature of constant notifications.

3. Prioritizing Notifications

Not all notifications are created equal. Prioritize notifications based on urgency and importance. Utilize features that enable categorization and filtering, allowing you to focus on critical messages while filtering out less essential information. This selective approach ensures that you remain informed without succumbing to information overload.

4. Utilizing Do Not Disturb Modes

Most devices offer "Do Not Disturb" modes, temporarily silencing notifications during designated periods. Leveraging these features can be instrumental in fostering uninterrupted focus, especially during crucial work hours or when engaging in deep, concentrated tasks.

Digital Detox Strategies

As the prevalence of digital communication continues to rise, the need for periodic digital detoxes becomes increasingly evident. Detoxing from the digital realm involves intentionally disconnecting to rejuvenate the mind, reduce stress, and regain perspective.

1. Scheduled Technology Breaks

Incorporate scheduled technology breaks into your routine. Designate specific time slots where you disconnect from all digital devices, allowing your mind to reset and recharge. Engaging in activities such as walking, meditation, or spending time in nature during these breaks can enhance the effectiveness of the detox.

2. Unplugging During Leisure

While online messaging has become integral to both professional and personal communication, it's essential to unplug during leisure time. Establish zones in your daily or weekly schedule where digital devices are set aside, fostering genuine, distraction-free connections with family and friends.

3. Mindful Consumption

Practice mindful consumption of digital content. Be intentional about the information you engage with, and set limits on the time spent scrolling through social media feeds. Uncontrolled consumption can contribute to the feeling of being overwhelmed by the digital landscape.

Conclusion

In the multifaceted landscape of online messaging, distractions pose a constant challenge to maintaining focus and productivity. By adopting strategic approaches such as managing notifications, setting boundaries, and embracing digital detox strategies, individuals can navigate the digital realm more effectively. Striking a balance between connectivity and intentional disconnection is key to harnessing the benefits of online messaging without succumbing to its distracting pitfalls. As we continue to explore the dynamics of online communication, understanding and mitigating distractions will be pivotal in shaping a healthy and productive digital experience.

Introduction

In the rapidly evolving landscape of communication, online messaging has become an integral part of our daily lives. The convenience and immediacy of digital communication platforms have transformed the way we connect with others, both near and far. While online messaging offers numerous benefits in terms of accessibility and connectivity, it also raises concerns about its impact on mental health. This article delves into the multifaceted dynamics of online messaging and its influence on our psychological well-being.

Positive Aspects of Online Messaging

1. Enhanced Connectivity

Online messaging breaks down geographical barriers, allowing individuals to stay connected with friends, family, and colleagues regardless of their location. This heightened connectivity can contribute positively to mental health by fostering a sense of belonging and reducing feelings of isolation.

2. Social Support Networks

Digital communication platforms provide a virtual space for social support networks to flourish. Individuals facing challenges or seeking advice can find comfort and assistance from friends or online communities. This support can have a protective effect on mental health, promoting resilience in times of stress.

3. Accessibility to Information

Online messaging facilitates the rapid exchange of information, empowering individuals with knowledge on mental health issues. Awareness campaigns, resources, and expert advice are easily accessible, promoting mental health literacy and reducing the stigma associated with mental health conditions.

Negative Aspects of Online Messaging

1. Digital Overload

The constant influx of messages and notifications can lead to digital overload, overwhelming individuals and contributing to heightened stress levels. The pressure to respond promptly can disrupt work-life balance and exacerbate anxiety.

2. Social Comparison and FOMO

FOMO stands for "Fear of Missing Out." It is a social anxiety stemming from the belief that others are experiencing enjoyable events or opportunities from which one is absent, often fueled by social media and the desire to stay connected with the activities of peers or the broader community.

Social media platforms often create an environment conducive to social comparison, where individuals compare their lives to curated online personas. This can lead to feelings of inadequacy and fear of missing out (FOMO), negatively impacting self-esteem and mental well-being.

Cyberbullying refers to the use of digital technologies, such as the internet and social media, to harass, intimidate, or harm individuals, often through the dissemination of hurtful or threatening messages, images, or other forms of online abuse. This form of bullying can have serious emotional and psychological consequences for the victims and is a growing concern in the digital age.

The anonymity provided by online platforms can lead to cyberbullying and harassment. Individuals may be subjected to negative comments, threats, or exclusionary behavior, resulting in significant psychological distress.

Strategies for Maintaining a Healthy Digital Balance

1. Set Boundaries

Establishing clear boundaries for digital communication is crucial. Designate specific times for checking messages and resist the urge to be constantly available. Communicate your boundaries to friends and colleagues to manage expectations.

2. Digital Detox

Periodic digital detoxes, where individuals disconnect from online messaging platforms, can provide a mental reset. This intentional break allows time for in-person interactions, outdoor activities, and self-reflection, contributing to improved mental well-being.

3. Mindful Consumption

Practice mindful consumption of online content by being selective about the information and interactions you engage with. Unfollow or mute accounts that contribute to negative emotions, and curate your digital environment to foster positivity.

4. Promote Positive Online Spaces

Actively contribute to creating positive online spaces by engaging in constructive conversations, supporting mental health initiatives, and reporting harmful behavior. Encourage empathy and kindness within your digital communities.

Conclusion

The impact of online messaging on mental health is a complex interplay of positive and negative factors. While the digital age has provided unprecedented opportunities for connectivity and information exchange, it has also introduced challenges that can affect our psychological well-being. Striking a balance between the benefits and pitfalls of online messaging is essential for maintaining a healthy relationship with digital communication.

Individuals can empower themselves by adopting strategies that promote a positive online experience and protect their mental health. Setting boundaries, practicing digital detox, and being mindful of online interactions are key components of a balanced approach to digital communication. Additionally, fostering a supportive and empathetic online community contributes to a collective effort to mitigate the negative aspects of online messaging.

As we continue to navigate the evolving landscape of communication technologies, it is crucial to prioritize mental health and well-being. By understanding the dynamics of online messaging and implementing strategies for a healthy digital balance, individuals can harness the benefits of connectivity while safeguarding their mental health in the digital age.

Introduction

In an era dominated by digital communication, the dynamics of online messaging have become integral to our personal and professional lives. As we immerse ourselves in the convenience and efficiency of instant messaging platforms, it becomes imperative to explore and understand the safety and security measures that can safeguard our digital interactions. This article delves into the essential aspects of online safety, focusing on encouraging strong passwords, implementing two-factor authentication, and adopting security best practices.

Encouraging Strong Passwords

The first line of defense against unauthorized access to our online messaging accounts is a robust password. A strong password is a cornerstone of online security, acting as a barrier between sensitive information and potential threats. To bolster this defense, it is crucial for users to follow best practices when creating and managing their passwords.

Creating a strong password involves a combination of uppercase and lowercase letters, numbers, and special characters. Avoiding easily guessable information such as birthdays or common words is essential to enhance the password's resilience. Additionally, regular password updates contribute to the overall security of online accounts, reducing the risk of compromise.

Educating users on the significance of unique passwords for each platform is equally important. Reusing passwords across multiple accounts increases vulnerability, as a breach on one platform could compromise multiple accounts. Encouraging the use of password manager tools can simplify the process of managing multiple complex passwords, promoting both security and user convenience.

Two-Factor Authentication

While strong passwords serve as a fundamental defense, implementing two-factor authentication (2FA) adds an extra layer of protection. 2FA requires users to provide a secondary form of verification in addition to their passwords, significantly reducing the likelihood of unauthorized access. This method typically involves receiving a code on a mobile device or using biometric authentication, adding an extra step to the login process.

Advocating for the adoption of 2FA is crucial in enhancing the security posture of online messaging platforms. Many messaging applications and email services offer 2FA options, and users should be encouraged to enable this feature whenever possible. Emphasizing the importance of securing the secondary authentication method, whether it be a mobile device or biometric data, is essential to maintaining the integrity of the 2FA process.

Ensuring Online Safety Through Security Best Practices

Beyond password strength and two-factor authentication, a holistic approach to online safety involves adopting security best practices that address a range of potential threats. This includes but is not limited to the following key considerations:

1. Regular Security Audits

Conducting regular security audits of messaging accounts is essential to identify and address potential vulnerabilities. Users should be educated on how to perform these audits and encouraged to review their security settings periodically.

2. Phishing Awareness

Phishing attacks remain a prevalent threat in the digital landscape. Educating users on recognizing and avoiding phishing attempts is crucial. This includes being cautious of unsolicited messages, verifying the authenticity of links, and avoiding the sharing of sensitive information through unsecured channels.

3. Device Security

The security of the devices used for online messaging is paramount. Users should be reminded to keep their operating systems and applications up-to-date with the latest security patches. Additionally, enabling device encryption and using reputable security software can further fortify the digital environment.

4. Data Encryption

Emphasizing the importance of end-to-end encryption in messaging platforms is essential for ensuring the privacy and security of conversations. Users should be informed about the encryption features of their chosen platforms and encouraged to use services that prioritize the protection of their data.

Platforms should implement robust user authentication mechanisms, ensuring that only authorized individuals have access to user accounts. Multi-step authentication processes, including challenge questions or biometric authentication, contribute to a more secure user authentication framework.

Conclusion

As we navigate the dynamic landscape of online messaging, prioritizing safety and security measures is non-negotiable. Encouraging users to adopt strong passwords, enable two-factor authentication, and adhere to security best practices creates a resilient defense against potential threats. The collaborative effort between users, platform developers, and security professionals is essential in fostering a secure online environment.

In conclusion, the exploration of safety and security measures in online messaging is not only a responsibility but also an opportunity to empower users with the knowledge and tools needed to protect their digital presence. By incorporating these measures into our digital routines, we can mitigate risks and enjoy the benefits of online communication with confidence and peace of mind.

The journey through the expansive terrain of online messaging has been a riveting exploration of the dynamics that shape our digital interactions. From the evolution of digital communication to the intricacies of online relationships, each chapter has unraveled a distinct facet of this complex landscape. As we bring this expedition to a close, let us reflect on the key takeaways and underline the significance of informed and mindful online communication.

Summarizing Key Takeaways

Our voyage began with an exploration of the roots and growth of online messaging, highlighting its indispensable role in contemporary communication. The convenience and accessibility offered by instant messaging across geographical boundaries emerged as a powerful force, transforming the dynamics of relationships with 24/7 connectivity. Global connectivity, the focus of another chapter, emphasized the importance of understanding cultural nuances in our digital exchanges, transcending physical borders to build meaningful connections.

Media sharing, examined in Chapter 4, illuminated how the exchange of photos, videos, and documents has enriched digital interactions, adding depth and emotion to our messages. However, the dependency on online messaging, as discussed in Chapter 5, comes with a cautionary note about the potential risks of over-reliance, urging a balance between virtual and face-to-face interactions for wholesome communication.

Miscommunication, explored in Chapter 6, shed light on the challenges of conveying emotions and intentions online. The strategies presented to minimize misunderstandings underscored the need for careful consideration of language and context in our digital exchanges. Chapter 7 delved into the realm of impersonal communication, urging users to address emotional nuances and build empathy through their online messages.

Privacy concerns, a critical aspect of our digital age, were dissected in Chapter 8, emphasizing the risks of message interception and data theft. The chapter on fraud prevention (Chapter 9) delved into the evolving techniques and challenges in safeguarding against online fraud. The complexities of cheating in digital relationships and the impact of online romance on personal lives were explored in Chapters 10 and 11, demanding a nuanced approach to fostering genuine connections in the digital realm.

The consequences of blocking, distractions, and their implications on mental health were discussed in Chapters 12, 13, and 14, respectively. Managing online interactions through blocking was presented as a double-edged sword, highlighting the risks and potential drawbacks. Distractions, often a byproduct of incessant notifications, prompted a discussion on digital detox strategies and the importance of maintaining productivity.

The impact of online messaging on mental health revealed a dichotomy of positive and negative aspects. While it facilitates connections and support systems, excessive use can lead to feelings of isolation and anxiety. Balancing the scales and adopting strategies for a healthy digital balance became imperative in this context.

In the realm of safety and security measures, explored in Chapter 15, the importance of strong passwords and two-factor authentication emerged as non-negotiable pillars of online safety. Encouraging users to adopt security best practices became a clarion call to protect oneself in the vast digital landscape.

Emphasizing the Importance of Informed and Mindful Online Communication

As we conclude our expedition, the overarching theme that resonates is the need for informed and mindful online communication. The digital landscape, with its myriad facets and intricacies, demands a conscientious approach from its inhabitants. The instant nature of online messaging often blurs the lines between intention and interpretation, necessitating a heightened awareness of our words and actions.

Understanding the cultural nuances and emotional subtleties embedded in digital communication is crucial. In an era where the world is at our fingertips, forging connections across borders requires a delicate balance of global awareness and local sensitivity. Media sharing, while enhancing the richness of our interactions, must be wielded with care, considering the impact on the receiver.

The dependency on online messaging, a natural consequence of its convenience, calls for a recalibration of our communication habits. While the digital realm offers unprecedented accessibility, the risks of over-reliance on virtual interactions cannot be ignored. Striking a harmonious balance between online messaging and face-to-face communication is the key to fostering genuine connections.

Miscommunication, a persistent challenge in the digital landscape, necessitates a proactive approach. Users must engage in clear and context-aware communication, employing strategies to bridge the gap between intention and interpretation. Impersonal communication, often a pitfall in the digital realm, can be mitigated through the cultivation of empathy and an understanding of emotional nuances.

Privacy concerns and the specter of fraud underscore the importance of vigilance in the digital space. Safeguarding personal information and adopting fraud prevention measures are integral to navigating the online landscape securely. Building on these foundations, the exploration of cheating in digital relationships and the complexities of online romance underscore the need for authenticity and transparency in our digital connections.

The ramifications of blocking, distractions, and mental health in the digital age call for a reflective pause. Users must be cognizant of the potential drawbacks of blocking and actively manage distractions to maintain productivity. The delicate balance between the positive and negative impacts of online messaging on mental well-being necessitates a thoughtful and measured approach.

In the realm of safety and security measures, the call to action is clear - empower oneself with the tools and knowledge to navigate the digital landscape securely. Strong passwords, two-factor authentication, and adherence to security best practices are not mere recommendations but essential pillars of online safety.

Conclusion

As we bid farewell to this exploration of the dynamics of online messaging, the key takeaway is clear - our digital interactions are a reflection of our choices, awareness, and responsibility. The vast and intricate landscape of online messaging offers unparalleled opportunities for connection, collaboration, and expression. However, it also demands a vigilant and thoughtful approach to navigate its complexities.

In conclusion, the journey through the chapters of this book has been a testament to the multifaceted nature of online messaging. From the evolution of digital communication to the intricacies of privacy and security, each aspect contributes to the rich tapestry of our digital interactions. As we step back from this exploration, let us carry forward the lessons learned, armed with the knowledge and mindfulness required to navigate the digital landscape with grace and resilience. Our online messages are not just words on a screen; they are bridges connecting us in a vast and interconnected world. May these connections be forged with intention, empathy, and an unwavering commitment to fostering a digital space that reflects the best of our humanity.

"Exploring the Dynamics of Online Messaging" delves into the heart of our interconnected world, unraveling the multifaceted layers of digital communication. From tracing the evolution and growth of online messaging to exploring its profound significance in contemporary communication, each chapter is a portal into a specific dimension of the digital frontier. The book navigates the convenience and accessibility of instant communication, examining its impact on relationships and global connectivity. It scrutinizes the challenges of conveying emotions online and the delicate balance between dependency and face-to-face interactions.

Engaging discussions unfold on media sharing, privacy concerns, fraud prevention, and the intricate landscape of digital relationships, including the advantages and disadvantages of online romance. With insights into the risks and consequences of blocking, strategies for managing distractions, and a nuanced exploration of the impact on mental health, the book offers a comprehensive guide. The concluding chapter ties together key takeaways, emphasizing the importance of informed and mindful online communication in navigating the digital landscape.

ABOUT THE AUTHOR

Mr. C. P. Kumar is a retired Scientist 'G' from National Institute of Hydrology, Roorkee, Uttarakhand, India. He is also a Reiki Healer and Chakra Balancing practitioner (with pendulum dowsing) and offers Emotional Freedom Technique (EFT) to help individuals with emotional issues. Mr. Kumar has authored many books on technical, spiritual, and social topics.

For further details, you may visit his webpage
https://www.angelfire.com/nh/cpkumar/virgo.html